Dr.

Mária Hanzséros,
Dr. Márta Pellérdi PhD

A relationship of loss

Introduction of Albee's world and a brief analysis of his *Who's Afraid of Virginia Woolf?*

VDM Verlag Dr. Müller

Impressum/Imprint (nur für Deutschland/ only for Germany)

Bibliografische Information der Deutschen Nationalbibliothek: Die Deutsche Nationalbibliothek verzeichnet diese Publikation in der Deutschen Nationalbibliografie; detaillierte bibliografische Daten sind im Internet über http://dnb.d-nb.de abrufbar.
Alle in diesem Buch genannten Marken und Produktnamen unterliegen warenzeichen-, marken- oder patentrechtlichem Schutz bzw. sind Warenzeichen oder eingetragene Warenzeichen der jeweiligen Inhaber. Die Wiedergabe von Marken, Produktnamen, Gebrauchsnamen, Handelsnamen, Warenbezeichnungen u.s.w. in diesem Werk berechtigt auch ohne besondere Kennzeichnung nicht zu der Annahme, dass solche Namen im Sinne der Warenzeichen- und Markenschutzgesetzgebung als frei zu betrachten wären und daher von jedermann benutzt werden dürften.

Coverbild: www.purestockx.com

Verlag: VDM Verlag Dr. Müller Aktiengesellschaft & Co. KG
Dudweiler Landstr. 99, 66123 Saarbrücken, Deutschland
Telefon +49 681 9100-698, Telefax +49 681 9100-988, Email: info@vdm-verlag.de

Herstellung in Deutschland:
Schaltungsdienst Lange o.H.G., Berlin
Books on Demand GmbH, Norderstedt
Reha GmbH, Saarbrücken
Amazon Distribution GmbH, Leipzig
ISBN: 978-3-639-10880-4

Imprint (only for USA, GB)

Bibliographic information published by the Deutsche Nationalbibliothek: The Deutsche Nationalbibliothek lists this publication in the Deutsche Nationalbibliografie; detailed bibliographic data are available in the Internet at http://dnb.d-nb.de.
Any brand names and product names mentioned in this book are subject to trademark, brand or patent protection and are trademarks or registered trademarks of their respective holders. The use of brand names, product names, common names, trade names, product descriptions etc. even without a particular marking in this works is in no way to be construed to mean that such names may be regarded as unrestricted in respect of trademark and brand protection legislation and could thus be used by anyone.

Cover image: www.purestockx.com

Publisher:
VDM Verlag Dr. Müller Aktiengesellschaft & Co. KG
Dudweiler Landstr. 99, 66123 Saarbrücken, Germany
Phone +49 681 9100-698, Fax +49 681 9100-988, Email: info@vdm-verlag.de

Printed in the U.S.A.
Printed in the U.K. by (see last page)
ISBN: 978-3-639-10880-4

TABLE OF CONTENTS

1. Introduction

The theatre and theatrical art have existed since the enlightenment of the human mind. At first, obviously, this "art" was manifested by primitive rituals, even when humans did not have the ability of speech. If we take the very first naive quasi-performances of cavemen into consideration, which are known from historic reviews and memories supplied by historians and archaeologists, their special motions, pagan customs, later their common dances, magicians' ceremonies, we can clearly recognise their aim for self-expression, their need for having contact with their gods, people, family -- with their audience, consequently.

The necessity to express one's life, religion, sorrow, happiness, political views, demonstration for and against society and its influence on people, led to the development of the theatre. There we, through actors, can experience all the above and so much more; a magic world which is still very real. This seems to be supported by the art historian, Gomlich, according to whom, "...drama originates in our reaction to the world, and not in the world itself." [1]

Alienation, depression, post-war disillusionment concerning human relationships: these feelings characterised the voices that appeared in the period beginning with the 20th century, one of whose representatives is Edward Albee. One of the main aims of this thesis is to introduce Albee's approach to the problems of his society, both in a social and private environment. It will be described how a marriage can fall apart in spite of the fact that both partners belong to the intellectual strata of the society, and also, how darkly they see the future, because it seems to be hopeless. The love that is perhaps between them will be questioned: it will be highlighted that this love is just a false feeling, just an illusion.

Illusion, passion, hatred and love: all these terms can refer to a relationship, even in an ordinary marriage. In Albee's *Who's*, the protagonists, George and Martha have experienced these extreme feelings and, despite the fact that both of them belong to the intellectual strata of the society, they cannot overcome their nihilistic life. The question as to why they are impotent in changing their life, why they are not strong enough to quit this marriage seems to be an enigma, but upon a closer look, this enigma can be revealed.

Hence, the other purpose of this thesis is to analyse George and Martha's partner-dependence, which results in the characters' losing their dignity and tolerance towards each-other. Also, the new and absurd ways of playwriting in the 1960s is introduced and highlighted, with emphasis on Albee and some of his contemporaries. A brief overview of Albee's first three-act play, *Who's Afraid of Virginia Woolf?* will be given. Also, a psychological background will be shown, making the partner-dependence of the two protagonists more clear.

Albee's predecessors, O'Neill, Williams, Miller, Ionesco and mostly Beckett had an impact on Albee's works, with their message, style and literary tools. Still, Albee created a new voice in drama. Naturally, in this analysis, the problems of Albee's age will also be shown. This play is an allegory of the American bitter feeling of life after the Second World War, when the past was shameful, the present had no meaning and the future was uncertain.

---

[1] Styan, <u>Modern</u>, Vol. 2., IX.

2. Albee and his predecessors

When talking about the common or different features and comparing Albee and his predecessors, Tennessee Williams and Arthur Miller, it can be seen that Albee is "less interested in guilt than responsibility, while at the heart of Miller's works "there is a concern with guilt, a guilt directly related to his experience as a Jew who had survived the Holocaust, and as an individual who had discovered his own potential for betrayal," while Williams is "hardly immune to charges of sentimentality, and desperate self-deceptions are practised by his characters".[2]

The American theatre at that time was eclectic. According to Wilmeth and Bigsby, "stylistic consistency" was missing, but its energy was based on the refusal of accepting conventional restraints. O'Neill uses "unstageable words", Williams exposes the "generative power of sexuality", Miller opens up the mind in such a way that he allows the self "to recreate the past and flow with freedom".[3]

Not only were the literary voices new, but the stage arrangement was a novelty, and the characters' way of speaking, behaving on the stage had changed. "Slurred and mumbling style of speech", "slouched stance", "hooded eyes", "the upper lip curled into sneer": this was the new image.[4]

Also, the behaviour of the characters changed: they were "losing control of the language: language as a means of communication evaporated and characters were increasingly unable to express ideas effectively or talk to each-other in meaningful ways".[5]

---

[2] Wilmeth and Bigsby, The Cambridge, Vol. 2., 5.
[3] Wilmeth and Bigsby, The Cambridge, Vol. 2., 6.
[4] Wilmeth and Bigsby, The Cambridge, Vol. 3., 112.
[5] Wilmeth and Bigsby, The Cambridge, Vol. 3., 112.

Edward Albee appeared on Broadway, and, more precisely, on Off-Broadway in the 1960s. After his one-act plays, *Who's* appeared and this was his first three-act piece. It ran for three and half hours, which must have been due to the meticulous elaboration of the play. It is interesting to note that the great amount of frank language and situations somehow frightened numerous producers.

The success of his play, first performed in the New York Billy Rose Theatre on 13 October in 1962, seemed to refute Eric Bentley, one of the most prominent American drama critic's view, according to whom:.

"There's no American drama. ... In America playwriting is not yet a profession. ...   Playwriting may be said to be a profession when playwrights of high average talent   are given their chance being production by performers who also constitute a profession. The American theatre does not offer playwrights this chance. A play cannot be produced on Broadway unless its producers think it is likely to run for a year".[6]

Maybe this statement is exaggerating to some extent, but the other side of the coin is that a play ran as long as tickets had been bought by the audience.

3. The Absurd

---

[6] Bentley, The Theatre , 7.

Certainly, the big rival, the movie attracted crowds of people in the sixties and the Broadway producers had to be careful with their choices of plays. Obviously, beside the financial, business-like features of theatre-making, something new and novel appeared in the life of Broadway, which was closely connected with the audience's new thinking. Life in its irrationality gave way to absurd, newly-shaped plays, which expressed disharmony in society, people's mental pessimism. This means that they were empty inside, without hope regarding the present and the future. Also, they were against the overall "Keep smiling!" slogan because they knew that this had been only a mask that people were suggested to wear. Behind this mask there was nihilism and disappointment.

The notion of the Theatre of the Absurd can be mostly connected to two famous names Samuel Beckett and Harold Pinter, and to a city: Paris. This capital became also the capital of dramatic art and gave place to surrealistic drama, the "theatre of the absurd", as it came to be known. Beckett's *En attendant Godot* (*Waiting for Godot*, 1952) and Ionesco's *Le Roi se meurt* (*Exit the King*, 1962) highlighted the beginning of this new period, which was also the period of the Cold War. As Styan states, these absurdists aimed to express the "futility of the world which seemed to have no purpose".[7]

To surprise or shock: these two aims could be seen and felt in absurd plays. For example, in Ionesco's play *Exit the King*, the main subject is death and the dissolution of the mind and body which is represented irrationally. Styan characterises these absurd plays as those that "fall within the symbolist tradition, and they have no logical plot or characterisation in a conventional sense"[8] and he adds that the characters are lacking motivation, with which their purposelessness is

---

[7] Styan, J. L., <u>Modern,</u> Vol.2., 125.
[8] Styan: <u>Modern,</u> Vol. 2., 126.

emphasised. There is no plot, and this is to suggest monotony, there is no communication, the dialogues have no real meaning. Interestingly, despite these strange features, the Absurd could find its way to the audience.

Albee made a distinction between the Realistic theatre and the Absurd theatre, as follows:

The Theatre of the Absurd... facing as it does man's condition as it is, is the Realistic theatre of our time: and... the supposed Realistic theatre ... pander[ing] to the public need for self-congratulation and reassurance and present[ing] a false picture of ourselves to ourselves, is ... really and truly The Theatre of the Absurd.[9]

Albee, like the European Absurdists, tried to dramatise reality, but while e.g. Beckett, Ionesco or Pinter shows reality in illogical absurdity, Albee "has been preoccupied with illusions that screen man from reality."[10] For Albee the world "makes no sense because the moral, religious, political and social structures man has erected to 'illusion' himself have collapsed."[11] In Albee's plays the audience always arrive at the recognition of reality behind illusion[12] and this is vital, because the confrontation can achieve its aim: the audience or the reader is not left in a dream-world.

Albee does not secede from reality in *Who's Afraid of Virginia Woolf?* Unlike Ionesco and Beckett, he does see some light at the end of the tunnel. Albee, although he also creates a hellish atmosphere in the play, between the lines and mostly at the end of the play it is not nihilism

---

[9] Cohn, <u>Edward</u>, 6.
[10] Cohn, <u>Edward,</u> 6.
[11] Cohn: <u>Edward,</u> 6.
[12] Cohn, <u>Edward,</u> 6.

that he aims to express. Instead, he gives a chance to his characters to continue their life in a more meaningful way.

4. To what extent is Albee absurd?

Martin Esslin, the critic, defined the plays of the absurd as "those that present man's metaphysical absurdity in aberrant dramatic style that mirrors the human situation".[13] The American "human situation" at that

---

[13] Stanton and Banham, <u>Cambridge</u>, 379.

time was interestingly deceiving: it was labelled as the American Dream, which meant an infinite variety of chances and fortunes, wealth and personal freedom. Yet, there was a veil separating the glittering appearance from the depressing reality. The notion of the American dream and its criticism have been a recurring theme of American literature because the 1960s was an era which was based on false ideas and deceiving slogans. This controversy had to be highlighted: using the absurd meant to expose these absurd relations. Market-oriented Broadway, and also Off-Broadway accepted the seemingly less profitable, new plays. These absurd pieces gained ground among intellectuals first because they were those people, who first understood the falseness of the "Keep Smiling!" policy. This might have meant smaller profit but the absurd movement proved to be a successful deal both financially and educationally. People had the ability to grasp the hidden or open meaning of absurd plays and they gradually got used to strange ways of expression and techniques, such as "... the rejection of narrative continuity, of character coherence and of the rigidity of logic, leading to ridiculous conclusions; scepticism about the meaning of language; bizarre relationship of stage properties to dramatic situation".[14]

We can call these features new-wave attempts: playwrights wanted to show reality in an unpolished, often naturalist, and thus in an (often) unpleasant way, neglecting prudery. To break off the "innocence" of the audience, Albee, after having finished *Who's Afraid of Virgia Woolf?*, said the following: "The play is an examination of the American scene, an attack on the substitution of artificial for real values in our society, a condemnation of complacency, cruelty, emasculation and vacuity; it is a stand against the fiction that everything in this slipping land of ours is

---

[14] Stanton and Banham: Cambridge, 379.

peachy-keen".[15] Consequently, Hayman states that *Who's...* "has something to do with the anguish of us all".[16]

It can be claimed now that a great deal depends on the philosophy of the writer. It makes a difference whether to accept and nourish nihilistic feelings or rather rage against something. It can be stated that Albee is only partly an absurdist writer. As Gspann writes, he rages against the society and not against life, as a whole.[17] We can have the impression that he leaves a little gate open to the characters, or to the audience, to be, if even secretly, optimistic. According to Bigsby, Albee is able to give a positive answer as to whether man can face reality and create values.[18]

The basic question that occurs here now is whether the world view or a special, philosophy, which is based on disappointment predestine the writer to be absurd or not. It is not necessary to become a priest if someone is religious. To use extreme tools to call attention to falsities, but remaining on real grounds suggest that instead of stressing nihilism, Albee suggests a solution or tries to give a chance to find the way out. As he claims, life is absurd in its own reality, and he thinks that the avantgarde theatre has liberating power: the audience will not forget the play while going home, in addition, these plays are not only useful but also entertaining as well.[19] Although Albee's previous pieces were also extraordinary and highly attracted the audience, still *Who's* was the real breakthrough, and a great triumph.

This successful play led to Albee's being called a "new Eugene O'Neill".[20] Since then, it has been debated whether Albee is an absurd

---

[15] Hayman, Contemporary, 44.
[16] Hayman: Contemporary, 44.
[17] Gspann, Edward, 25.
[18] Gspann, Edward, 25.
[19] Gspann: Edward, 52
[20] Kazin, Writers, 31.

writer or not. His earlier plays, for example the *Zoo Story, The Sandbox* and *The American Dream* contain absurd features. Still, *Who's* lacks those typical, "traditional" features that are characteristic of the absurd.

The absurd is a theater genre that aims to mean plays performed in "out of harmony".[21] The "leaders" in this style were mostly Beckett, Adamov, Ionesco and Genet, but, according to Esslin, Albee and Pinter were less absurd in their works than the former artists.[22] If reading through *Who's,* it can be clearly seen that the play is absurd because life is absurd, but still lacks those typical elements that characterise absurd pieces. The absurd techniques involve the "rejection of narrative continuity, of character coherence and of the rigidity of logic, leading to ridiculous conclusions; scepticism about the meaning of language; bizarre relationship of stage properties to dramatic situation."[23]

Albee's absurdism in this play lies between the lines, and it is the language of the play which bears absurd features. The quick, short, sarcastic exchange of words often remind the reader of the Beckettian language:

GEORGE: Good Lord, Martha ... do you know what time it ... *Who's* coming over?
MARTHA: What's-their-name.
GEORGE: Who?
MARTHA: WHAT'S-THEIR-NAME!
GEORGE: Who what's-their-name?[24]

---

[21] Stanton and Banham, Cambridge, 379.
[22] Stanton and Banham, Cambridge, 379.
[23] Stanton and Banham, Cambridge, 379.
[24] Albee, Who's, 14.

When the Beckettian influence is mentioned, it is not by mistake. Albee himself claimed that he considered Beckett to be his tutor, although the great predecessors, Williams and O'Neill also set examples for Albee.

As for Albee, the idea of his topic in *Who's* was influenced by absurdist features, although in this play there *is* a plot and there *is* communication, but these "ingredients" correlate with the lack of motivation in his characters. What is meant by this is that the relationship of George and Martha takes place in real circumstances, in a seemingly ordinary background, but we might even take their humanly empty communication as a lack of communication as well. However, when we talk about motivations, we mean positive actions, thinking, leading to somewhere. In *Who's* the protagonists' only motivation is to destroy each-other, consequently, this kind of motivation leads nowhere and this is how Albee's play reflects a nihilistic atmosphere. (But, in the very last scene George and Martha might be showing us their real faces: they reveal *feelings* towards each-other, and, as we have already experienced, Albee here gives them a ray of hope.)

Albee's aim, thus, was not a kind of soothing art that reflected illusion: he gave the viewer a virtual slap by showing them a counter-example through George and Martha's and Honey and Nick's way of life. Albee, in an interview with Patricia DeLa Fuente put his opinion straight: "Art is not a pacification. It's disturbance. Art should shock a lazy, complacent audience back to life ... I don't think you should frighten them, I think you should terrify them."[25]

It cannot be a mere coincidence the George works at the History Department: he and, consequently, his (our) history cannot solve the period's heavy problems. His figure can be the allegoric example for this vacuum. He, who used to be a hopeful talent, could not fullfill anybody's expectation: neither his wife's, nor his father-in-law's, and, first of all, his own expectations had gone up in smoke, too.

Beckett, Ionesco, Pinter and other absurdists, present "reality in all its alogical absurdity. Albee has been preoccupied with illusions that screen man from reality".[26] Still illusion is present in Albee's plays, "the process of collapse is often dramatised and thus the audience can recognise the reality behind the illusion", claims Cohn.[27]

If we turn to the idea that drama is based on our instinct of imitation, the trace that is followed by Albee in this play is the imitation of social feeling and behaviour in a figurative sense. The success of this play lies in this merit: the audience can recognise themselves and the ill-state of their society. Also, through the influence of the play, they can recognise their own problems and the play makes them think over their relationships, too.

5. Some psychological aspects of *Who's*

The starting point of the play *Who's* is based on a very basic theme: husband-wife relationship in marriage. As life does not exist without compromises, a marriage cannot maintain itself without a mutual give-and-take. Even in partnerships where there is no love, a sensible agreement can save human dignity. In *Who's* this very fundamental element is totally missing. The protagonists, George and Martha, spend a whole life by repressing their wishes and desires. They play a game of having a child, which, seemingly, satisfies both of them. Their dream,

---

[25] Kolin, Conversations, XIII.
[26] Cohn: Edward, 6.

which is false, reflects the artifice of the society around them. Between four walls they are able to kill and adore each-other. Outside the walls they wear a mask of pretence. This inside-outside unfitting splits their psyche.

Splitting in psychiatry[28] means an asymmetry of the mind, a duplicated thinking develops, which results in false decisions: George and Martha know they do not have a son but they cannot face it, so they escape to an imaginary parenthood. Their splitting, which is unconscious, blocks their will from accepting reality and from making steps towards a life-like solution. An ill partner-dependence has arisen. The great danger of splitting is that the one, who suffers from it, cannot solve the problems he escapes from, although he tries to find an answer. It is usually a split person who chooses the easy, e.g. unreal solution, which seems to be satisfactory and which gives tranquillity -- on the surface. Naturally, the figure of these two protagonists is merely symbolic, they can be regarded as a typification. Through them, private and social problems can be followed.

Jung states that "Everything that should normally be in the outer attitude, but is conspicuously absent, will invariably be found in the inner attitude. This is a fundamental rule...".[29] This rule is the "homeostatic rule of self-regulation"[30] and it is "the means by which all organic systems keep themselves in a state of balance, despite changes in the environment".[31] According to this statement, George and Martha must have the ability to reveal their very true self but since they lie even to themselves, their relationship and their way of living is a psychiatric case.

---

[27] Cohn, Edward, 6.
[28] Consultation: Dr. Péter Szentesi, head physician, Halfway Centre, Budapest.
[29] Stevens, Jung , 54.
[30] Stevens, Jung, 54.

Comparing their artificial behaviour and mental state and, for example, Kasey's figures in *One Flew over the Cuckoo's Nest*, the apparent difference is that while George and Martha do not want to know about their illness, Kasey's protagonists, the "real" insanes, *want* to leave their lunacy behind because they accept help. Our "heroes" accept neither each-other's help, nor their own strength. Their escapism to a dream-world just deepens the gap between them and between their capabilities of fulfilling their tasks in life. As absurd is this catch, as "out of harmony" is their behaviour.

Albee first wanted to give the title *Exorcism* to this play, but he changed his mind and Act Three received this title. The dependence on the fantasy is exorcised[32] especially in this act, but this is the case throughout the whole play. He changed the title later to the present one, maybe because he did not want to reveal the gist. This choice of the title creates a less rough approach to the plot, suggesting that apart from George and Martha's ill symbiosis and relationship, the audience is given an opportunity to handle their hell in a less straightforward way. "Exorcism" may reflect the writer's pessimism, while the final title is ambiguous in the sense that without knowing the exact content of the play, the audience is left by with an open question, thus suggesting that there are two different ways to comprehend the problem arising in the play.

Humour and allegories also arise in this play. Gspann claims that some critics were unsatisfied with the allegory of the c*hild*, saying that an educated couple would not be able to cherish such an illusion.[33] The central figure of the child was questioned by quite many critics, because they do not really comprehend the necessity of such a solution in the

---

[31] Stevens, Jung:,54.
[32] Hayman, Contemporary, 34.

play. Gspann writes that according to critic Tom Driver, the play is about four homosexuals because such an illusion, like an imaginary child, can happen only between homosexuals. Another critic, Charles Morowitz draws a parallelism between the child and Albee's private life. According to Morowitz, the child does not haunt George and Martha, on the contrary, it haunts the adopted child, Albee.[34]

Alan Schneider, the director of the very first performance of the *Who's* gave an answer to these remarks. He says that Albee's play is not about the child, and if the figure of the child is just a trick, then "so is our unfanthomable friend, Godot".[35] Godot, who never appears on the stage but still exists: he exists because Vladimir and Estragon know about him and wait for him. He gives hope, because he is waited for and he could change the lives of those people, who wait for him, like God(ot). The illusory child will never come but still exists in his "parents'" mind, thus also giving hope -- the same way as Godot's coming would give a ray of sunshine to those who wait for him. The role of Godot and the child is similar, it expresses people's desires, hopes and belief in a better future. The problem is, though, that Godot never comes, although he exists, and the child never comes because he does not exist. Still, the child can be a kind of solution, who could save a marriage or who could show a way out of George and Martha's empty marriage.

As for the dialogues, Albee followed the Beckettian style in some parts, thus supporting the idea that quarrelling is, among others, only a displacement activity for George and Martha. Many symbols in the play are based on Tennessee William's and Dürrenmatt's influence, and absurd humour is also present. Albee is not sentimental but the illusion here is present and he gives a kind of freedom for his characters to

---

[33] Gspann, Edward, 70.
[34] Gspann, Edward, 82.

15

chose, unlike Beckett, for instance, whose characters cannot move freely.[36]

All in all, the play can be considered as an allegory of contemporary American society through the life of an ordinary American family. On the contrary, Richard Schechner claims that *Who's* is really a classic: the classic of bad morals, naturalism and morbidity, without action. He adds that the play shows a false picture of contemporary American society.[37] Most of the critics praise Albee's talent in his linguistic solutions, his sense of humour, his rhythm. To answer the question whether this play is an absurd one or not, it is considered that although Albee creates an absurd situation, his literary tools are life-like and still human-like. The sad reality is, though, that an absurd situation like George and Martha's constant quarrel could happen to anybody, while in the case of Godot, the play is only a virtual reality. It can be suggested that the play is modern, bearing absurd features but it is not uniquely absurd.

---

[35] Gspann, Edward, 83.
[36] Gspann, Edward, 80.
[37] Schechner, Who's, 7-10, 63-64.

6. The characters

Martha and George are the main figures in the play but their one night guests, Honey and Nick also have an important role. Martha and George's marriage relies upon a false, deceptive, unhealthy relationship, it can be stated that this is not a relationship at all, because if two people's only "joy" is to torment each other, it is not a "traditional"marriage, which lies upon respect. They just have a relationship, which is empty and full of disgrace.

As the title of the three acts indicates: *Fun and Games, Walpurgisnacht*, and finally the *Exorcism*, these three steps may highlight the three steps of their own life. Supposedly, at first their relationship and marriage was true and loving, then *something* happened and their partnership became worse and worse. Now they are enemies but the sad fact is that neither of them wins in this battle. Both of them virtually die in their meaningless fight with each other, they lose their personality, their soul and innocence. *pychic victory*

To understand what happened in the past, the reader or the audience must go back in time. Martha, as the daughter of the Dean of the local university, and the promising talent, George, working for the History department, could not or were unable to fulfill the requirements of their public, and their private lives. The shadow of the father and George's temperament, which lacks pushy, careerist features, creates a collision between the partners. Neither of them can attain happiness because both of them are unsuccessful in their public life. This disturbing reality slowly penetrates into their relationship and causes a never-ending tormenting of each other.

What is also noticeable is that although they virtually try to kill each other, they do have an illusion: a child, who exists only in their minds and thoughts. Still, this illusory child connects them, although this is the only illusion that may show that they still preserve a little part in their soul about their long forgotten love. They live a life between truth and illusion and this is deceptive: instead of facing the fact that taking an illusion for real leads to a dream world, which does not give an answer to their real problems, they stick to an unreal phantasm.

Here occurs a question, however, whether Albee wanted to indicate the false institution of marriage in general in the US, or, whether he wanted to introduce the then American overall trend, the "American dream", which was just an illusion too.

Stenz suggests that "their illusory child represents an attempt to explore the success or failure of American revolutionary principles" because George and Martha are named after George and Martha

Washington..[38] On the other hand, Albee's view about this question is as follows, when asked about the invention of an imaginary son:

[...] it always struck me as very odd that an audience would be unwilling to believe that a highly educated, sensitive, and intelligent couple, who were terribly good at playing reality and fantasy games, *wouldn't* have the education, the sensitivity, and the intelligence to create a realistic symbol for themselves.[39]

Marriage as an institution covers "self-delusion, materialism, opportunism and cannibalism".[40] The word "cannibalism" shows exactly what is going on between the protagonists. They suck each other's blood, like vampires and they do it during a hellish night. Martha is the dominating person in the battle. She is older than her husband and she is fierce: she burns herself and everybody around her. She attacks and when she behaves normally, in a minute she changes back to her attacking position. The truth behind all this is that she aims to humiliate George completely, criticising him and giving him orders:

MARTHA [pause]: Well, what's the name of the picture?
GEORGE: I really don't know, Martha...
MARTHA: Well, think!
GEORGE: I'm tired, dear ... it's late ... and besides ...
MARTHA: I don't know what you're so tired about ... you haven't *done* anything all day: you didn't have any classes, or anything ...
GEORGE: Well, I'm tired. ... If your father didn't set up these goddamn Saturday night orgies all the time ...

[38] Stenz, Edward, 38.
[39] Kazin: Writers, 338.

MARTHA: Well, that's too bad about you, George ...

GEORGE [grumbling]: Well, that's how it is, anyway.

MARTHA: You didn't *do* anything; you never *do* anything; you never *mix*. You just sit around and *talk*.

GEORGE: What do you want me to do? Do you want me to act like you? Do you want me to go around all night *braying* at everybody, the way you do?

MARTHA [braying]: I DON'T BRAY!

GEORGE [softly]: All right ... you don't bray.

MARTHA [hurt]: I do not *bray*.

GEORGE: All right. I said you didn't bray.

MARTHA [pouting]: Make me a drink![41]

It can be seen that this "Make me a drink!" (request? order?) shows that the word "please" is missing from Martha's dictionary. She also lacks the basic living together rules. She invites guests for the night without telling about it to her husband. Moreover, it is upon the pressure of her father that she does so:

MARTHA: You remember them now?

GEORGE: Yes, I guess so, Martha ... But why in God's name are they coming over   here now?

MARTHA [in a so-there voice]: Because Daddy said we should be nice to them, that's why.

GEORGE [defeated]: Oh, Lord.

MARTHA: May I have a drink, please? Daddy said we should be nice to them. Thank you.[42]

---

[40] Stenz, Edward, 38.
[41] Albee, Who's, 13.

What is interesting to note is that now Martha is behaving according to her father's wish, she could find words like *please* and *thank you*, as if the thought of her father made her nicer. Perhaps these two polite words mean that she is unable to fight with her father. She fights with her husband instead. Psychologically, it is understandable: she obeys the shadow of her father, she sticks to her father's requirements and this way she sacrifices her life.   As for George, who is a learned man and used to be a promising talent, one can have the impression that he somehow bends under Martha's vulgarity, hysteria and aggression. In reality, George is a volcano, it is only his manners that save him from reaching the same level as Martha's. This behaviour is apparent in the first act.

According to Stenz, Martha's treatment of George is "the emotional castration of the male by the female in American society, and Martha's dissatisfaction does not go beyond the fact that George lacks a public relations personality."[43]

It is hardly possible to imagine how these two people could fall in love at all. They are so different now. They might have been tolerant and loving to each other in the past though. It can be stated that, as time went by, George could not or simply did not want to respond to Martha's energy. This energy can derive from sexuality. At this moment both of them are frigid towards each other and this can be due to the lack of love. It is hardly believable that these two people love each other. They have a relationship, they live together but, in spite of the fact that there can be such strange marriages, where the two partners kill each other but still love each other, it is hardly believable that George and Martha

---

[42] Albee, Who's, 14.
[43] Stenz, Edward, 39.

love each other. As it has been mentioned, they are likely suffering in a partner-dependance, which is rather an illness than love.

As it was stated before, some critics led debates about the question of sexuality in *Who's*, believing that the play is about four homosexual males.[44] Albee again gave an answer to these:

Indeed, it is true that a number of the movie critics of *Who's Afraid of Virginia Woolf?* have repeated the speculation that the play was written about four homosexuals disguised as heterosexual men and women. This comment first appeared around the time the play was produced. I was fascinated by it. I suppose what disturbed me about it was twofold: first, nobody has ever bothered to ask *me* whether it was true; second, the critics and columnists made no attempt to document the assertion from the text of the play. The facts are simple: *Who's Afraid of Virginia Woolf?* was written about two heterosexual couples. If I had wanted to write a play about four homosexuals, I would have done so.[45]

Returning to the couple, in their younger years they must have behaved differently to each other. Either careerism or a kind of mental problem, a misunderstanding of the institution of marriage led to their sterile relationship, but it is possible that the lack of a real child is the main reason of their strange behaviour. To imagine a child is a displacement activity, just like torturing each other and consuming huge amounts of alcohol, especially in Martha's case. *escapism*

Martha is a victim, but she can hardly see this. She, as a powerful woman "is discouraged by family, education and society from having

---

[44] Gspann, <u>Edward,</u> 82.
[45] Kazin, <u>Writers,</u> 331-332.

personal goals".[46] She does not possess any self esteem, she tries to prove something but it is clear even for herself that by giving up her desires in connection with her husband becoming the head of the History department, or bearing a child, she is on the way toward destroying herself. It is strange that she cannot see it. This is her destiny: she is unable to recognise that sometimes turning to somebody for help can save lives and hopes. In addition, she is fifty-two and she cannot accept the fact that she is growing old. Surely, it must be frustrating for her that George is eight years younger. It is interesting to remark, though, that despite this age difference and their serious problems, George does not want anybody else but Martha. It can be stated that they know or feel that they must stay together because they need each other. This is their crucial and central trap.

---

[46] Stenz, Edward, 40.

7. Act One: Fun and Games

In this play, it is interesting to note that, according to Gspann, the dialogues lead to the past and thus the reader understands a great deal from the facts that were hidden so far.[47] This statement is true because the night that the two couples spenf together starts with George and Martha's usual quarrel and kidding. In the beginning the audience knows nearly nothing about that couple. What they can see is that these two people enjoy torturing each other. What they should do is get rid of a large amount of self deceit. The notion of this deception grows and grows as the play proceeds, so the audience get involved into this strange atmosphere step by step. As Gspann claims, their living room is the symbol of hell, and these two have already tortured each other to their deepest part of their soul, by sucking even the marrow from each other's bones.[48]

If the reader compares the physical features of the characters, it can be seen immediately that even the physical differences are blatant. Martha, is a "large, boisterous woman"[49], looking younger than her age, and her ample figure is right the opposite of her thin, grey haired, younger husband. This difference can be seen in their behaviour as well:

---

[47] Gspann, Edward, 56.
[48] Gspann, Edward, 56.
[49] Albee, Who's, 9.

Martha is more vulgar and louder than her husband, who is calmer but is not a give in character either.

Their guests, Nick and Honey are the couple of the future, a kind of continuation of the ageing protagonists. Honey is plain, blonde and in many ways stupid. Her husband, Nick, is handsome and has a muscular body. In the Honey-Nick couple opposite forces can be seen: while Martha is the leading voice, it is Nick who dominates in his marriage.

They might be considered to be just "another unhappily married couple"[50], but their first names allude to Martha and George Washington, "America's first presidential couple"[51], who were also childless. Also, according to Albee, "they represent an American type: a bitter, alienated couple, bored with themselves and each other".[52]

Sometimes the reader gets a different impression than the writer's opinion. Hence, it can be stated that Martha and George are not only a bored couple. They want to fill in a gap between each other in their marriage: there is a secret between them that nobody knows, and this is their imaginary son.

The play is based on four characters, but the focus is on the relationship of George and Martha "who express their love in a lyricism of witty malice".[53] Cohn also claims that although they torment each-other, "they need one another -- a need that may be called love".[54]

Now, Wilson and Cohn are of a different opinion, including Albee. On the one hand, Albee considers his heroes to be a bored couple, and does not mention love at all, but on the other hand Cohn finds love behind the never-ending torment. Cohn calls George and Martha a

---

[50] Wilson, The Theater, 194.
[51] Wilson, The Theater, 194.
[52] Wilson, The Theater, 194.
[53] Cohn, Edward, 18.
[54] Cohn, Edward, 18.

"dissonant duet"[55] and also, by the end of the play they reach " a hint of communion".[56]

Scrutinising Act One, the reader cannot discover any hint of love, though. On the contrary. When Martha *wants* a kiss, George coldly turns her down:

MARTHA: Hello. C'mon over here and give your Mommy a big sloppy kiss.

GEORGE: ... oh, now ...-

MARTHA: I WANT A BIG SLOPPY KISS!

GEORGE [preoccupied]: I don't *want* to kiss you, Martha. Where *are* these people? Where are these *people* you invited over?

MARTHA: They stayed on to talk to Daddy .... They'll be here ... *Why* don't you want to kiss me?

GEORGE [too matter of fact]: Well, dear, if I kissed you I'd get all excited ... I'd get beside myself, and I'd take you, by force, right here on the living-room rug, and then our little guests would walk in, and ... well, just think what your father would say about *that.*[57]

At the end of this awkward conversation the figure of Martha's father again appears. He is the fifth character in this play, although he never appears on the stage. Still, his personality has always been there, between them, dominating their marriage. He was the one who had forbidden George to publish his novel. This father killed George's hopes, George and Martha also kill each other and they really do it by words. Somehow death is always behind their words and actions. Their love died, their desires died, even their illusory child dies -- their whole life

[55] Cohn, Edward, 18.
[56] Cohn, Edward, 18.

can be considered to be like a survival game. To symbolise this, in the First Act George shoots Martha with a toy gun, but it might make the audience imagine that he might do it with a real gun as well, in the storm of their quarrels:

[George takes from behind his back a short-barrelled shotgun, and calmly aims it at the back of Martha's head. Honey screams ... rises. Nick rises, and, simultaneously, Martha turns her head to face George. George pulls the trigger.]

GEORGE: POW!

[Pop! From the barrel of the gun blossoms of large red and yellow Chinese parasol. Honey screams again, this time less, and mostly from relief and confusion.]

You're dead! Pow! You're dead!

NICK [laughing]: Good Lord!

[Honey is beside herself. Martha laughs too ... almost breaks down, her great laugh booming. George joins in the general laughter and confusion. It dies, eventually.]

HONEY: Oh! My goodness!

MARTHA [joyously]: Where'd you get that, you bastard?

NICK: [his hand out for the gun]: Let me see that, will you?

[George hands him the gun.]

HONEY: I've never been so frightened in my life! Never![58]

The above piece proves what crazy thoughts can appear in George's head. To put a rifle against anybody is a really childish or really serious deed. The reader can understand it though. These two men,

---

[57] Albee, Who's, 17.
[58] Albee, Who's, 41.

27

George and Martha are really enemies, like in a war. What is ridiculous is, that the whole company laughs at this situation and Honey screams like a baby and her fear is shown by a really silly sentence. She has never been so frightened in her life, which can be true, but still, this sentence from her sounds childish and ridiculous.

Now that the guests are all together, it is again because of Daddy's request. George and Martha's fragile family peace is disturbed. In other words, Daddy rules again. Hence, George and Martha are not independent people. They depend on Daddy, and in an unhealthy sense, on each other. Subconsciously they might have enough of this dependence but neither of them is strong or brave enough to break out.. Instead, they keep torturing each other, and consuming lots of alcohol. "Live and let die!" could be their slogan.

The couple's only activity is to play a silly and cruel game of words. These words lack any kind of tolerance:

> MARTHA [after a moment's consideration]: You make me puke!
> GEORGE: What?
> MARTHA: Uh ... you make me puke![59]

In the First Act, *Fun and Games*, when they appear on the stage, it is clear that they hate each other. It can be two o'clock at night or daylight, but these two people simply keep scolding each other. Although this rage ceases by the morning, the reader cannot know, for how long the ceasefire will last.

The opinion of those analysts, for example Cohn, who claim that these two people somehow love each other, might be questioned. True love does not survive in nihilism and the purposeful hunting of the other.

Love cannot exist between two people who do nothing but torment one-another. If it is love, then it is a strange, unnatural feeling, labelled as love. How could there be any love between those who communicate as follows:

MARTHA: ... I mean, you're a blank, a chiper ...

GEORGE: ... and try to keep your clothes on, too. There aren't many more sickening sights than you with a couple of drinks in you and your skirt up over your head, you know...

MARTHA: ... a zero. ...[60]

Erich Fromm claims that those who are unable to develop their total personality, will fail. He adds that if their love towards people is missing, self-love cannot give satisfaction.[61]

George and Martha do not love each other and they do not love anybody. Each of them tries to push their personality ahead, leaving behind the respect of the other. They cannot live the life of a middle aged, normal, settled married couple. They do not believe in their past and present, not to mention their scepticism, and their future. According to Gspann, they are in antagonistic symbiosis and Martha symbolises the consuming attitude of their age.[62] She is vulgar, chews ice cubes, she is not a feminine character at all. She has the body of a woman but she has the mind of a stuck up, drunken female. When their visitors ring the bell and she orders George to open the door, her only remark on George's unwillingness is a short, vulgar sentence: "Screw you!"[63]

---

[59] Albee, Who's, 16.
[60] Albee, Who's, 18.
[61] Fromm, A szeretet, 7.
[62] Gspann, Edward, 57.
[63] Albee, Who's, 19.

George's intellectual aestheticism, however, dominates. Martha is the embodiment of barbarism, sometimes she speaks like a little girl, acts like one who is immature mentally and emotionally, as well.[64] However, she feels disgust toward herself, that is why she always tries to prove something that covers her self criticism.

It is true that Martha's way of speaking sometimes resembles the speech of a young girl, but her aggressive manners dominate. Where and when did she lose her feminine character? In the past, at the beginning of their marriage they must have been full of emotions and care. As years went by, they gradually got stuck into a dream life. As neither of them could get what they aimed to achieve (Martha did not become a mother, George did not run a career), they blame each other for these failures. Instead of strengthening each other, they virtually kill each other. The reader or the audience can have the feeling that only one more step is needed for a physical scuffle to take place on stage.

As it has been mentioned, most critics consider the couple to be a symbol of the American standards, from the social point of view. The feeling of life at that time covered disappointment, after the Second World War people did not see the future and in the shade of the atomic bomb and the destruction it caused shocked millions of people. Their present and future was hopeless and disillusionment reigned people's life. This disillusionment can be felt in George and Martha's life, too. They do not believe in future. Their empty relationship is an allegory of the nihilistic feeling of their age. But, according to Gspann, Martha is first of all Martha, and her figure of a burnt out middle-aged American intellectual is only a secondary feature.[65]

---

[64] Gspann, Edward, 57.
[65] Gspann, Edward, 58.

On the other hand, Albee stresses their typicality of the American type of people, saying that "the play is likely about the decline of the West".[66]

Although it seems that Martha's only aim is to destroy people around her, George's character is a little pale and he withdraws into the smoke of his cigarette. Still, he has kept some of his individuality. He is not as harsh as his wife and when they are in a verbal conflict, he heroically defends himself. The problem is that the atmosphere that Martha creates is murderous and everybody who becomes involved with her, somehow becomes ordinary and base. George would get on well with his books and with his life, although it is a bitter feeling for him that he did not become the head of the History Department. The reader has the impression that George would be able to handle his life. On the other hand, Martha is a troublemaker, she blames George for missing a brilliant career. If Martha were intelligent enough to understand what is behind George's life that he chose, instead of progress in his work, she would notice that she herself was a part of this choice. Demanding all the time instead of giving and understanding is not fair, this is why Martha does not have the right to call George to account for anything.

It is Martha who rebels but she does it for the sake of rebellion. She can scold George or she can be unsatisfied, she can be the leader in their conversations, yet she is alone. Martha might be aware of this, and that is why she extends her rage upon others, except for one person, her Daddy. She is completely dependent upon Daddy. (Whom she calls "Daddy" as a child.) She wants to fulfill Daddy's requirements and she would like George to do the same.

In the First Act, it can be realised immediately that all the four people are prisoners of a closed world, they are empty. The university

---

[66] Gspann, Edward, 58.

town, called New Carthago, is the place where, according to the Bible, love is dirty. Interestingly, the puritan university environment is the seedbed of promiscuity.[67] George senses, still, that New Carthago will fall.

When Nick and Honey arrive, George and Martha continues their strange behaviour in front of the newcomers. All the more, Martha tries to force their own unsuccessful view of life on the guests. Martha, as she calls their guests "kids" shows that she cannot accept other people's dignity. In this game George takes part, too. It is noticeable though that when George digs back into his memories of his courting, he changes tone and speaks in a friendly way, although he changes back his tone quickly, maybe realising that he was sentimental.

Martha is also strange: when she is addressed "lady-like", she refuses such nice adjectives, demanding her "rubbing alcohol".[68] She does not want sentimentalism and refuses care.

According to Gspann, the two guests function as a catalyst in the relationship of George and Martha.[69] As for physical features, the new couple is just the opposite. Nick's body is sportish, George's is not. Honey is simple, and has a childish personality, and thin hips. Nick and Honey also call Daddy a remarkable man and Martha agrees. During the First Act the audience cannot hear any positive adjective which would be addressed to George.

Although, at first sight Nick and George are so different in their physical stature, there is still a similarity between the two men. This similarity lies in their way of life. Nick is a promising talent but his future might be the same as George's, when he becomes middle aged. If Nick

---

[67] Gspann, Edward, 59.
[68] Albee, Who's, 22.
[69] Gspann, Edward, 60.

cannot fulfill the expectations of Daddy or any other professors in the university, he will lose all his dreams, too.

His wife, Honey, is very simple and she is also in the trap of careerism. Her desire for a career is in connection with her husband's career -- one can see the future when Nick does not fulfill the requirements, she will lose her interest in her husband. The life of the two pairs is partly about carreerism and repressed sexuality. Honey does not want a child, that is why she and her husband might avoid intercourses, Martha and George are so much stuck in their fight that they hardly feel any sexual affection for each other. They repress their sexuality, they cannot turn towards each other with clear affection. Subconsciously, their body is against this "turning away". Furthermore, none of them foster sincere feelings to each other..

It has already been mentioned that the "ghost" of Martha's father is always floating above them:

GEORGE: [...] Martha's father expects loyalty and devotion out of his ... staff... to cling to the walls of this place, like the ivy ... to come here and grow old ... to fall in the line of service [...][70]

This father is a real person, contrary to another figure, George and Martha's imaginary son. Gspann claims that this son is the symbol of their sterility and self deceit.[71] What is again unfair from Martha is that she mentions this son to Honey. She has not known Honey before, she has not talked about their "son" to anybody before, so why now? It can be claimed that her action again was addressed against George. Perhaps Martha wants to prove again that she can do anything with

---

[70] Albee, Who's, 31.
[71] Gspann, Edward, 61.

George's soul, she can hurt him again, but she does not consider the consequences. Or, as *Fun and Games* is the title of Act One, she just wants to play a game by mentioning their secret, But, it is deeply unwise to use illusion as a weapon against somebody:

> HONEY [to George brightly]: I didn't know until just a minute ago that you had a son.
> GEORGE [wheeling, as if struck from behind]: WHAT?
> HONEY: A son! I hadn't known.
> NICK: You to know and me to find out. Well, he must be quite a big...
> HONEY: Twenty one ... twenty one tomorrow ... tomorrow's his birthday.
> NICK: [a victorious smile]: Well!
> GEORGE [to Honey]: She told you about him?
> HONEY [flustered]: Well, *yes*. Well, I mean ...
> GEORGE [nailing it down}: She told you about him.
> HONEY [nervous giggle]: Yes.
> GEORGE [strangely]: You say she's changing?
> HONEY: Yes ...
> GEORGE: And she mentioned ...
> HONEY [cheerful, but a little puzzled]: ... your son's birthday... yes.
> GEORGE [more or less to himself]: O.K., Martha ... O.K.[72]

It can be stated that Martha wanted to destroy George by revealing their mutual secret. She does not know that in this way she punishes herself, too. George had the feeling at the beginning that this was going to happen and threatened Martha not to talk about it. It is typical of her that although George warned her twice not to mention their "secret", she deliberately does the opposite. She provoked George, maybe because she wanted George to feel small and defeated by her, or maybe she wanted a scandal, thus showing their guests her power again. The other reason might be that now she can talk about a thing that has never been mentioned before to strangers:

GEORGE: Just don't shoot your mouth off ... about ... you-know-what.

MARTHA [surprisingly vehement]: I'll talk about any goddamn thing I want to, George![73]

The problem is that Martha speaks about the son because she wants to put George into an awkward situation. It is not a brave behaviour, especially since she does this not because she wants to get rid of an illusion. Martha's "confession" is damaging, rather than interesting.

Some critics did not fully understand the role of the child. They considered it to be a "false part in the play".[74] According to Hayman, "childlessness works as a symbol of emotional and spiritual sterility".[75] To balance this sterility, they have invented a child, and now, this balance is in danger.

---

[72] Edward, Who's, 33-34.
[73] Albee, Who's, 25.
[74] Gspann, Edward, 62.
[75] Hayman,Contemporary, 30.

Through the whole of Act One, however , the reader can witness some humour. When George and Martha are not killing each other, they are teasing each other. This is strange in the eye of their guests. Cohn claims that this evening is different from George and Martha's other evenings. Martha spoke about their son, and "once revealed, their son must die".[76]

However, it can be a debated question whether the son must or must not die. George and Martha could have played their game with this idea of a child without killing him. Sadly, it is in their veins to destroy each other, consequently they destroy their mutual dream.

The audience, during the First Act, and through the whole play gets a great deal of slang and loose conversations. A middle-aged couple is seen on stage who does not know what to do with their life: to make a compromise, to hurt, to treat their guests as guests or humiliate them as well. Unfortunately, Act One does not suggest a happy outcome: the whole atmosphere is irritating and nerve wracking.

8. Act Two: Walpurgisnacht

In this act, the strange night continues. While the two women are out of the room, making coffee, the two men try to converse, but George's sarcastic temperament dominates their talk.

George, with his witty malice, makes Nick confess about his wife's pregnancy alarm. This was a false alarm, but they got married, because

---

[76] Cohn, Edward, 20.

36

Nick wanted to prove that he did not want to leave Honey alone under these circumstances.

While the two men talk, the reader can have a break from the war between George and Martha. The atmosphere at the beginning of this act is not so hectic. Hence, there is a disturbing conversation between the men and it is George, who teases Nick. But, there is a big difference between them, too. When they run out of ice, Nick's only problem is to have some more.

When George tells the story of a boy who had killed his family, neither Nick, nor the reader is sure whether this story is based on reality or not. During this night nothing is certain.

As for Gspann, the story, in which the murderer boy is put into asylum in the end, can be a symbol of George's insane marriage. The boy became mute, and this allegorises George's literary silence.[77] Nick just listens and tries to guess whether this is again a game or not.

It turns out also that Nick married Honey partly because of her money. Here there is a difference again between them: George married in an "old fashioned" way, that is not for money, but because of love. The reader now is in doubt and confused: if George had such sincere feelings, how is it that he could not preserve a part of that sincere feeling for the present? It can be stated, on the contrary, that he may have sincere feelings somewhere deep inside towards his wife, his usage of words sometimes contain "love", but mostly he is under the pressure of Martha, who is really a beast and this behaviour prevents George from showing emotions, provided he still has any.

In this act the central problematic event is their dance. Honey, who does not understand much of the things that are around them and those

---

[77] Gspann, Edward, 67.

actions that influence the whole evening, wants to dance. This is a good occasion for Martha to start flirting with Nick:

> HONEY [all sweetness again] [To Martha] : Oh, I'm so glad ... I just love dancing. Don't you?
> MARTHA [with a glance at Nick]: Yeah ... yeah, that's not a bad idea.[78]

From this *glance* the reader can feel that something dirty is going to happen. The ageing Martha, either for fun, or for the sake of making George feel a zero, starts flirting with Nick. Nick, partly because he got excited but partly because he is not brave enough to say no to the daughter of the Dean, gradually melts under the influence of Martha. The others are just watching them, but Albee again puts some humour into this situation:

> MARTHA: I like the way you move.
> NICK: I like the way you move, too.
> GEORGE: [to Honey]: They like the way they move.[79]

It is obvious that George does not take the other two's dance seriously on the surface. He knows that Martha is doing it just to make him and the others shocked. But in Martha's behaviour there is more than just trying to make others shocked. She wants to make her husband jealous. It can be added though, that the strange behaviour of Martha is rather frustrating. In the place of George, most men would

---

[78] Albee, <u>Who's</u>, 78.
[79] Albee, <u>Who's</u>, 81.

have divorced long time ago. They are still together, despite Martha's dirty games.

Interestingly, it is not Martha's flirting that hurts George deeply. His rage breaks out when Martha tells the others that the story about that boy, who killed his family is not really just a book by George, but it is his own story. The bomb explodes. The worst thing is that Daddy's figure appears again, he, who did not allow the publication of this book:

MARTHA: Georgie said ... but Daddy... I mean... ha, ha, ha, ha ...but *Sir*, it isn't a novel at all ... [Other voice] Not a novel? [Mimicking George's voice] No, sir, ... it isn't a novel at all ...

GEORGE [advancing on her]: You will not say this!

NICK [sensing the danger]: Hey.

MARTHA: The hell I won't. Keep away from me, you bastard!

[Back off a little ... uses GEORGE's voice again]

No, Sir, this isn't a novel at all ... this is the truth ... this really happened ... TO ME!

GEORGE [on her]: I'LL KILL YOU![80]

At that very moment, the disaster of the fight happens, they start to struggle. It is ridiculous that Nick, George and Martha start fighting, but it is understandable from the point of view of the fact that Martha betrayed George again. As George later remarked, they had played the Humiliate the Host game. To some extent it is a little boring sometimes that these two people do nothing but find out silly games to torture each other.

This was not enough for them, anyway. There comes now the "Get the Guests" game, which is for humbling their guests. When reading about this never ending battle, it is still a question why the guests still stay on. It can be a subconscious interest about the outcome of the night, it can be Martha and George's influence, and maybe their behaviour can seem to be sort of interesting to the others. Or, Nick and Honey are stupid and simply cannot make up their minds to leave.

In spite of the clear difference between the two couples from an educational point of view, in reality neither George, nor Martha is any different from Nick and Honey. It is true that Honey stays with Nick because he is the man of the future in the university, but she does not hurt him openly. It is hard to decide which is a bigger lie, to stay together in hatred or to stay together for interest.

As mentioned, the Get the Guests game is the next game, proposed by George. According to Stenz the "Get the Guests game is to punish Nick for his mindless complexity in Martha's degradation of him and he exposes the young Biology Instructor as a conceited self-righteous career builder."[81]

As the happenings carried on, and George nearly killed Martha by grabbing her throat, and after the Get the Guest game, it is clear that something more serious must happen, not physically, but mentally. As Martha and George cannot hold themselves back either in connection with each-other, or in connection with their guests, it can be sensed that they have to be sentenced to lose something very valuable. Since they cannot behave and cannot think intelligently, however educated they might be, they deserve punishment. Before that, they declare a "total war" upon each other.

When Martha is out in the kitchen playing sex games with Nick, Honey confesses that she does not want a child, it is only George, who tries to think over this whole confusion. Honey thinks she heard the bell

---

[80] Edward, Who's, 83.
[81] Stenz, Edward, 50.

ring, and this gives an idea to George, an idea, which is fatal for him and for Martha.

GEORGE [he is home now]: ... somebody rang ... it was somebody ... with ... I'VE GOT IT! I'VE GOT IT, MARTHA ...! Somebody with a message ... and the message was ... our son ... OUR SON! [Almost whispered] It was a message ... the   bells rang and it was a message, and it was about ... our son ... and the message ... was ... and the message was ... our ... son ... is... DEAD![82]

As he had enough of this illusion but is also afraid of this new situation, he calls his wife laughing and crying at the same time. After declaring total war, "George knows that he has to do it irrevocably to change their lives".[83]   A child, even imaginary, holds together their marriage. Stenz points out that "the link which this couple manufacture in the form of a fantasy child is an ultimate irony in a relationship rife with disillusionment and guilt. The childlessness of George and Martha is a blessing in disguise; a real infant born into their marriage would have been born into the unholy cauldron of his mother's and his father's unresolved personal and emotional problems".[84]

The above statement can really be true. This game with the imaginary child is even better than to have a real one, in the case of George and Martha. The fact that George has enough and "kills" their child, their illusion, is the most sensible deed. George senses that this can be their only escape now: an escape to reality.

---

[82] Albee, Who's, 107.
[83] Stenz, Edward, 50.

9. Act Three: The Exorcism

This act begins with Martha's monologue. There is nobody on the stage, and this fact can be allegorical, too. Martha, alone, has to face her life and when she is left alone, her words are true and without rage. It seems that, under the surface, she has already accepted that her father is a dictator. She now calls him "Daddy White Mouse"[85], the same way George called him before. She mentions his red eyes, too, because "he cries all the time, and so does she and so does George".[86] All of them have a reason to cry, but mostly George and Martha. Their life has been

---

[84] Stenz, Edward, 51.
[85] Albee, Who's, 109.
[86] Hayman, Contemporary, 41.

spent in a twenty-one-year-long self deceit, a dream or illusion. Now Martha is getting to grasp that a turning point is coming, she feels it in her bones. Maybe this is why she changes tone, when alone.

The audience does not know what would have really happened to her and Nick if they had not drunk so much alcohol. All in all, their sexual intercourse did not happen and now, when Nick enters the stage, Martha tells him the truth, that it is only George who has ever made her happy:

MARTHA: ... George who is out somewhere there in the dark. ... George who is good to me, and whom I revile; who understands me, and when I push off; who can make me laugh, and I choke it back in my throat; who can hold me, at night, so that it's warm, and whom I will bite so there is blood; who keeps learning the games we play quickly as I can change the rules; who can make me happy and I do not wish to
be happy, and yes I do wish to be happy. George and Martha: sad, sad, sad.

NICK [echoing, still not believing]: Sad.

MARTHA: ... whom I will not forgive for having come to rest; for having seen me and having said: yes, this will do; who has made the hideous, the hurting, the insulting mistake of loving me and must be punished for it. George and Martha: sad, sad, sad.[87]

This time Albee is not ironical. Martha means what she says. This confession does not belong to their games. It comes from deep inside and that is why these words are true.

According to Gspann, this confession is important because it makes it possible for Martha and George to find each other again.[88]

[87] Albee, Who's, 113.
[88] Gspann, Edward, 75.

There is a little chance for these two miserable people to get closer to each other's hearts.

Martha's attitude has changed and now she considers Nick to be the houseboy. Now Nick has the same role (opening the door when the bell rings) as George had in the first act. The reader can see that Nick got what he deserved: for money and career he would do anything, but now his personality is visible. Gspann draws a parallelism between Nick and George and Martha's "son": had they had a son, it is possible that he would have become a "houseboy"-like figure, like Nick.[89]

This is just an assumption though. Life could have given them another chance. It is possible that if they had had a son, their whole life would have turned into another direction. In a lot of marriages it is the child that holds the parents together. In George and Martha's case it might have happened differently. They would have had meaning in their life. Now they have their silly, dangerous games with one another and with others. All these games are just displacement activities to fill in their empty lives.

The games, however, must go on. George enters with flowers (snapdragons). "Flores; flores para los muertos. Flores."[90] These flowers are partly a present for Martha and the flowers are for the grave of their son."[91] According to Gspann, this Latin quotation is derived from Tennessee Williams's *A Streetcar Named Desire*. These flowers are symbols, and George hides himself and his pain behind the flowers. As for Hayman, also, this Latin sentence foreshadows that George will kill the son.[92]

---

[89] Gspann, Edward, 76.
[90] Albee, Who's, 115.
[91] Gspann, Edward, 76.
[92] Gspann, Edward, 76.

When George starts throwing the snapdragons on Nick and Martha, this is much more "violent" than when he shot Martha with the toy gun. The toy gun game was just a game, but throwing the flowers at her means a farewell to their dreams, it is the beginning of the last game that George proposes, "Bringing Up Baby". Martha senses that this very last game will be the cruellest one, her tone is nearly tender, but George insists:

MARTHA [a sleepy child]: No more games ... please. It's games I don't want. No more games.

GEORGE: Aw, sure you do, Martha ... original game-girl and all, 'course you do.

MARTHA: Ugly games ... ugly. And now this new one?

GEORGE [stroking her hair]: You'll love it, baby.

MARTHA: No George.

GEORGE: You'll have a ball.

MARTHA [tenderly; moves to touch him]: Please, George, no more games; I ...

GEORGE [slapping her moving hand with vehemence]: Don't you touch me! You keep your paws clean for the undergraduates![93]

For this last game Honey is needed. George and Martha is playing a role, the role of parents and how they brought him up. This part of the play is tender. The very sad and equally the most interesting lines: the "memories" of their child-rearing, the nice and loving words now mean that this is the last time that the two spouses can speak about their son.

---

[93] Albee, <u>Who's</u>, 122.

In the meantime, George is reciting in Latin from the burial service, "interpolating his lines into Martha's narrative about the imaginary past.[94]

The "performance" of the two is so suggestive that Honey, who was deliberately invited to take part in the last game, starts to cry for a baby. Maybe she feels the nicety of being a mother. One would think, though, that this is only the heat of the moment. Little Honey, in reality, does not want any children because she is so plain and simple, without any significant features.

This very last game culminates in George's speech saying their son died in an accident. Martha and George speaks simultaneously. Martha tells how she "tried to protect their son from 'the mire of this vile, crushing marriage', while George is reciting in Latin. It is now that he kills the boy off."[95] Martha's reaction is horrible:

GEORGE: Martha ... [Long pause] ... our son is ... dead.

    [Silence.]

    He was ... killed ... late in the afternoon ...

    [Silence.]

    [A tiny chuckle] on a country road, with his learner's permit in his pocket, he swerved, to avoid a porcupine, and drove straight into a ...

    MARTHA [rigid fury]: YOU ... CAN'T ... DO ... THAT!

    GEORGE; ... large tree.

    MARTHA: YOU CANNOT DO THAT![96]

The rest of the story, that the postman brought a telegram with the sad news and that George ate the letter, is after this climax. Albee is

---

[94] Hayman, Contemporary, 43.
[95] Hayman, Contemporary, 43.

satirical in this part of the conversation between George and Martha. It is interesting that even in the saddest moment, at the very moment when they are finished with their illusion, Albee does not dramatise.

What is dramatic is that Nick finally understands what is going on. "Very quietly and simply, he gives George and Martha a chance to confess the truth:"[97]

> NICK [to GEORGE; quietly]: You couldn't have ... any?
> GEORGE: *We* couldn't.
> MARTHA [a hint of communion in this]: *We* couldn't.[98]

This confession, the mutual secret revealed, made the couple get closer to each other. Now the audience has understood all the quarrels, the games, the kidding and the hellish provocations: behind all this there lies the truth that this couple is sterile. But now they do not say that George or Martha is to blame for this sterility. They both take up the responsibility, they do not point at each other. Maybe this *"We* couldn't" mutual confession is one of the most sincere sentences between the George and Martha through the whole play. Because it is true. This is their mutual pain and they would not have survived if they had not covered the surface of the problems.

The final scene, after the guests have left is human, slow and intimate. In each other's arms they are alone, without their dream, their illusion. It is Saturday morning, the beginning of a new day. They are afraid of Virginia Woolf, the big bad wolf, which destroys illusions; but they are stronger now and their head is clear. They are for each other and the little gate is still open to them: to have a nicer future than their

---

[96] Albee, Who's, 135.
[97] Hayman, Contemporary, 43.

past. One day both of them will understand why that boy had to die: to let them live in the real world.

10. Albee and his critics

In 1959, the American theatre was in "desperate need of a change and Albee the young man supplied it".[98] This view about the need for theatrical change is also supported by the writer himself: "People were sort of waiting for this new generation of the American theatre, so it was an ideal time for us to come along"[100]. -- said Albee, the rebel, who, together with other artists "attacked the psychological realism of an earlier decade and in its place established the avant-garde".[101]

Albee's avantgardism was manifested in the use of new topics with a new language, turning to abstractions and polarizations in an absurdist-naturalist manner. Being an avantgardist, he freely created and

---

[98] Albee, Who's, 138.
[99] Kolin, Conversations, VIII.
[100] Kolin, Conversations, VIII.
[101] Kolin, Conversations, VIII.

supported the newest ideas and techniques in his art. Furthermore, his friend, William Flanagan characterised Albee as a "sort of complete man of the theatre".[102] His completeness means that he did not only write plays but he also directed his and other writers' works, and he did all these "with precision and grace".[103] He was a "cultural hero"[104], and, apart from his angry young manhood he was also the cultural ambassador for the US State Department.[105] His unbroken popularity and "reign" in theatrical circles were praised by Tennessee Williams as well: "I've a great feeling for Edward Albee. I've never seen any play of his that I didn't think was absolutely thrilling. He is truly a major playwright, America's major playwright".[106]

We have seen before that Broadway was very sensitive, as regards plays to be put on stage, and mainly for financial reasons. Albee's *Who's* proved to be a big commercial success. Due to his theatre successes, Albee was interviewed by critics several times and his appearance was often paralleled with his inner world, sometimes in a half-serious, half-humorous manner. Critic Marilyn Preston released an article in which she described his look: "It's almost absurd for him to look so boyish, so benign. A writer's anguish should show on his face. For someone so distinguished, who writes so well and speaks so sincerely about human pain and suffering and existential kvetchiness, Albee's face is remarkably clean and unblemished. With freckles, he could do cereal commercials".[107]

While critics (sometimes) tried to put emphasis on his figure ("handsome, lean, dark-haired young man with a crew cut and

---

[102] Kolin, <u>Conversations,</u> VIII.
[103] Kolin, <u>Conversations,</u> VIII.
[104] Kolin, <u>Conversations,</u> IX.
[105] Kolin, <u>Conversations,</u> IX.
[106] Kolin, <u>Conversations,</u> VII.
[107] Kolin, <u>Conversations,</u> IX.

considerable charm..."[108]), or draw a parallelism between his personality and one of his characters ("... who talks very like George in *Who's Afraid of Virginia Woolf?*: a low, cultivated, almost brooding speech with a flair for sudden wit or a mildly cynical comment"[109]), Albee preferred wit and humour, but he did not consider himself a writer of jokes. "Any writer without a sense of humour is suspect."[110] -- he says. About *Who's* he confided that "it was a comedy in the sense that everybody ended up with what they wanted".[111]

This "comedy" directed by Alan Schneider, ran 663 performances on the Broadway, starring Uta Hagen, Arthur Hill, George Grizzard (later Ben Piazza), and Melinda Dillon. The ovation and respect it gained by the audience and by the critics won him the Outer Circle Award, but he was "denied the Pulitzer Prize for the play even though he was recommended for it".[112] It was the language and the subject matter that were objected to. A contemporary critic, J. D. Maxwell considered it to be a "filthy" play[113].

Yet, the 1964 London premiere of *Who's* gained another award, the Evening Standard Award, for the writer. At the time he did not direct the play, but years later, in the Broadway three-month revival of the performance in 1976, it was Albee who took over the role of the director, thus following his "tradition" of directing his own plays, as he had done it before in the case of his *Seascape* in 1975 in New York in the Shubert Theatre. Not only did he direct his and other writers' plays but he also dealt with adaptations, such as Gile Cooper's play, *Everything in the*

---

[108] Kolin, Conversations, IX.
[109] Kolin, Conversations, X.
[110] Kolin, Conversations, XV.
[111] Kolin, Conversations, XV.
[112] Kolin, Conversations, XXIV.
[113] Kolin, Conversations, XXIV.

Garden, which ran 84 performances at the Plymouth Theatre in New York in 1967.[114]

Albee's versatile personality and wit brought him successes and full houses in every theatre. The play *Who's Afraid of Virginia Woolf?*, however, was banned in Johannesburg in 1963, due to Albee's objection to segregation..[115]

The importance of this play is significant because its thought-provoking message could reach the reader or the audience by making them look inside their souls, thus making them recognise the falseties of life and relationships that seem to be glittery from outside. Also, the play indirectly introduces the American social reality. It shows that those hectic problems that can be found in the society, can be found in relationships and thus these partnerships become empty and full of disappointment. In George and Martha's case there is no promising future with great changes, but maybe by returning to reality they will be able to face their life and might generate a more valuable future for themselves. It is indisputably the merit of the play that it sticks to reality and offers a way out for his main characters, George and Martha.

---

[114] Kolin, Conversations, XXV-XXVII.
[115] Kolin, Conversations, XIII.

11. Conclusion

Edward Albee, "the king of Off-Broadway"[116] conquered Broadway in 1962 with his first all-night-long play, the *Who's Afraid of Virginia Woolf?* The premiere took place on 13 October, 1962 in the Billy Rose Theatre and it ran 663 performances.[117]

The reason why this play was so successful is that it is not only a new wave production, but also it exposes two things at the same time. Albee partly symbolises the American overall depression through the characters and their life, but he partly confronts the viewer with themselves through the psychological drama of two married couples. The audience or the reader recognises the falseties of life, even their own life, in a willy nilly way.

That alienation and depression that characterised the 1960s America gave the idea to Albee to write this three act play, after some one act pieces. He wants to confront the viewer with the illusions that ruled the era. The play is about illusion, anger and hatred, George and Martha's constant fight with each other, involving their night guests, Nick and Honey. Parallelism can be drawn between the two couples in a way that the continuation, the next generation in the person of Nick and Honey will not be better than the ageing George and Martha. Still, George and Martha have kept some values of the past, but Nick and Honey's figure and behaviour suggests that careerism and empty partnership will characterise the new generation.

The question whether there is still love in its real sense between the partners in interesting to analyse. The partnership between Nick and

---

[116] Gspann, Edward, 55.
[117] Gspann, Edward, 55.

Honey is purely based on financial grounds and carreerism. On the contrary, George and Martha cherish some love toward each other, but as years went by, this love turned into a feeling that can be called partner-dependence. This is not a healthy condition, in spite of their very last sincere and emotional conversation, when they get back to reality after killing their "son".

The play whirls with great power through all the three acts, revealing barbarism in human feelings and unveiling untrue ambitions. Sentimentalism is not shown at all. The excellence of Albee is that although the topic is tragic, he used humour as well to avoid total naturalism.

As for the first production, Albee chose Alan Schneider to be the director, and the producers were Richard Barr and Clinton Wilder.[118] These people had already directed plays by Beckett, Pinter and Genet. Their names and the very well written *Who's* attracted crowds of people in the Billy Rose Theatre and later all over Europe. Albee visited Hungary, too, and the reception of this play was also a big success on Hungarian stages as well.

Although the *Who's Afraid of Virginia Woolf?* was written in the 1960s, its message is still valid. It fights against nihilism in human relationships, it confronts the present day readers with their pitiful desires. The play stresses that although an illusion can maintain relationships for a while, these relationships become true only if the partners turn to reality and are strong enough to grasp that a dream world leads nowhere. The play suggests that the only way out of the swamp is to face the truth of life,.

---

[118] Gspann, Edward, 55.

Bibliography

Albee, Edward, 2001, Who's Afraid of Virginia Woolf? London, Vintage.

Bentley, Eric, 1968, The Theatre of Commitment, London, Methuen and Co.

Cohn, Ruby, 1969, Pamphlets on American Writers, No. 77., Minneapolis, University of   Minnesota Press.

Fromm, Erich, 1993, A szeretet mûvészete, Budapest, Helikon.

Gspann Veronika, 1992, Edward Albee drámái, Budapest, Akadémiai Kiadó.

Hayman, Ronald, 1971, Contemporary Playwrights. Edward Albee, London, Heinemann.

Interview: 5 July, 2005, Dr. Péter Szentesi, head physician, Halfway Centre, Budapest. (Ms.)

Kazin, Alfred, 1968, Writers at Work. The Paris Review Interviews, London, Martin Secker and Warburg Limited.

Kolin, Philip, 1988, Conversations with Edward Albee, USA, University Press of Mississippi.

Schechner, Richard, 1963, Who's Afraid of Edward Albee? Tulane Review, VIII.

Stanton, Sarah and Banham, Martin, 1996, Cambridge Paperback Guide to Theatre, Cambridge, Cambridge University Press.

Stenz, Anita M., 1978, The Poet of Loss, The Hague, Mouton Publishers.

Stevens, Anthony, 1996, Jung, Oxford, Oxford University Press.

Styan, J. L., 1992, Modern Drama in Theory and Practice, Vol. 2., Cambridge, Cambridge University Press.

Wilmeth, Don B., and Bigsby, Christopher, 2000, <u>The Cambridge History of American Theatre</u>, Vols 2,3., Cambridge, Cambridge University Press.

Wilson, Edurin, 1985, <u>The Theater Experience,</u> USA, McGraw Hill Co.

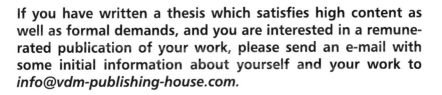

Printed in Great Britain
by Amazon

50296528R00038